ShowTime® Piano

Disney

LEVEL 2A

Arranged by Nancy and Randall Faber

This book belongs to: _____

Production Coordinator: Jon Ophoff
Editor: Isabel Otero Bowen
Design and Illustration: Terpstra Design, San Francisco
Engraving: Dovetree Productions, Inc.

FABER
PIANO ADVENTURES®

Hal•Leonard®

A NOTE TO TEACHERS

ShowTime® Piano Disney brings together contemporary and classic Disney hits arranged for the pianist at Level 2A. In Walt Disney's words, "There is more treasure in books than in all the pirates' loot on Treasure Island." This book offers musical treasure for piano students with blockbusters from *Coco, Pirates of the Caribbean, Mulan, The Little Mermaid, Mary Poppins, The Princess and the Frog*, and more.

Students develop confidence at the piano through reading basic rhythms, notes, intervals, and simple chords. ShowTime Piano books explore these fundamentals with fun, appealing songs.

ShowTime® Piano designates Level 2A of the PreTime to BigTime Supplementary Piano Library arranged by Faber & Faber. The series allows students to enjoy a favorite style at their current level of study. ShowTime books are available in these styles: *Popular, Classics, Jazz & Blues, Rock 'n Roll, Ragtime & Marches, Hymns, Kids' Songs, Christmas*, and the *Faber Studio Collection*.

Visit us at **PianoAdventures.com**.

Teacher Duets

Occasional optional teacher duets are a feature of the ShowTime Piano series. The arrangements are complete on their own, with duets providing a fullness of harmony and rhythmic vitality. This gives the teacher, parents, and more advanced students the opportunity to play together.

Helpful Hints:

1. The student should know his or her part well before the duet is used. Accurate rhythm is important!

2. Rehearsal numbers are provided for convenient starting places.

THE PRETIME TO BIGTIME PIANO LIBRARY

PreTime® Piano   =   Primer Level

PlayTime® Piano   =   Level 1

ShowTime® Piano   =   Level 2A

ChordTime® Piano   =   Level 2B

FunTime® Piano   =   Level 3A–3B

BigTime® Piano   =   Level 4 & above

ISBN 978-1-61677-699-2

Printed in U.S.A.

TABLE OF CONTENTS

FF3041

4

WHO SAID THIS?
Ariel, please! Will you get your head out of the clouds and back in the water where it belongs?

Under the Sea
from *THE LITTLE MERMAID*

Music by ALAN MENKEN
Lyrics by HOWARD ASHMAN

Moderately fast

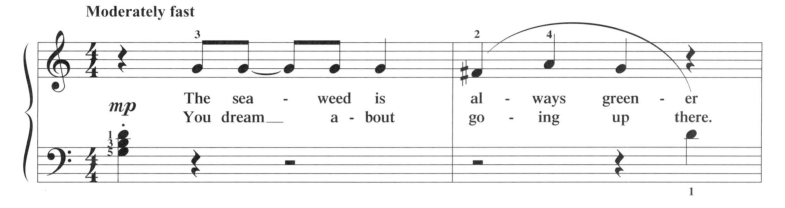

mp

The sea - weed is al - ways green - er
You dream___ a - bout go - ing up there.

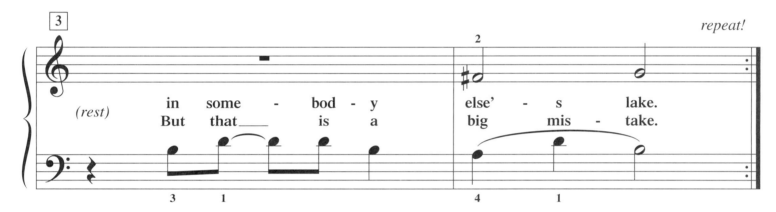

repeat!

(rest) in some - bod - y else' - s lake.
But that___ is a big mis - take.

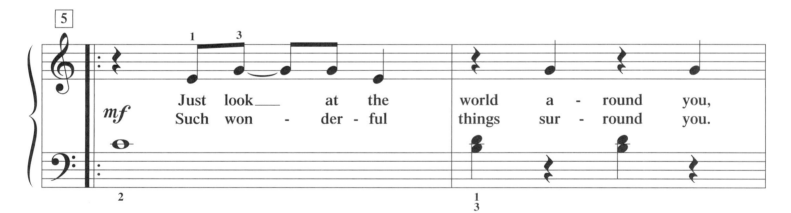

mf

Just look___ at the world a - round you,
Such won - der - ful things sur - round you.

repeat from measure 5!

right here___ on the o - cean floor.
What more___ is you look - in' for?

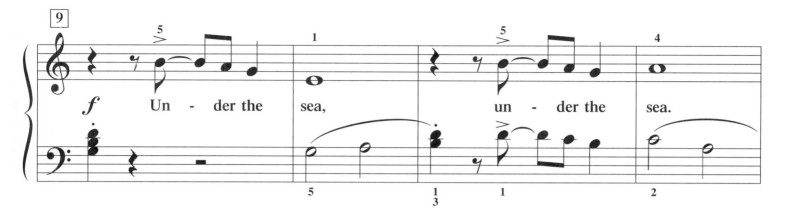

9

Un - der the sea, un - der the sea.

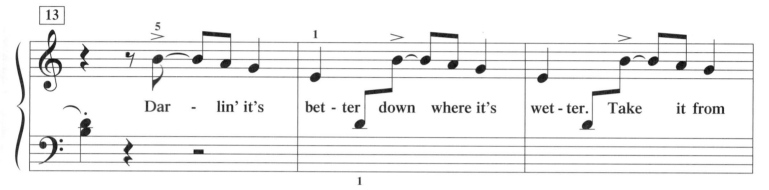

13

Dar - lin' it's bet - ter down where it's wet - ter. Take it from

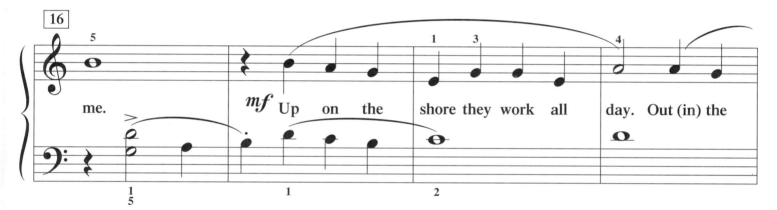

16

me. *mf* Up on the shore they work all day. Out (in) the

20

sun they slave a - way. While we de - vo - tin' full time to

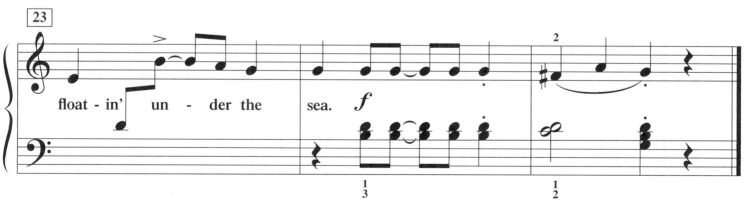

23

float - in' un - der the sea. *f*

WHO SAID THIS?
In every job that must be done there is an element of fun.

Chim Chim Cher-ee

from *Mary Poppins*

Words and Music by
RICHARD M. SHERMAN
and ROBERT B. SHERMAN

Cheerfully

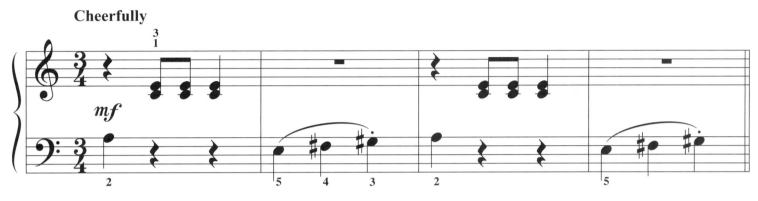

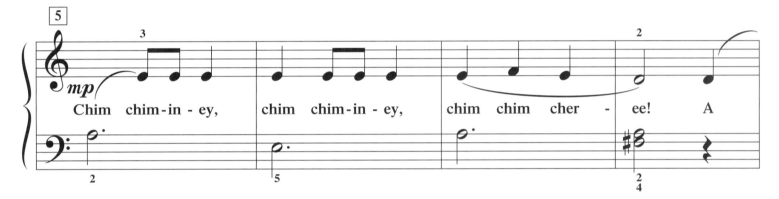

Chim chim-in - ey, chim chim-in - ey, chim chim cher - ee! A

Teacher Duet: (Student plays 1 octave higher)

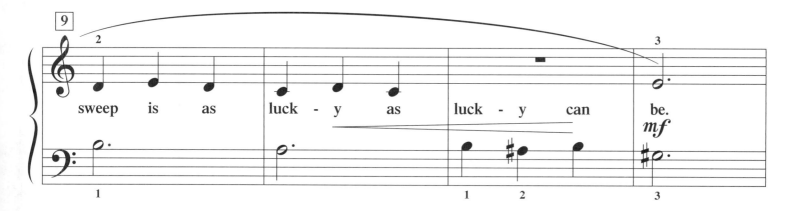

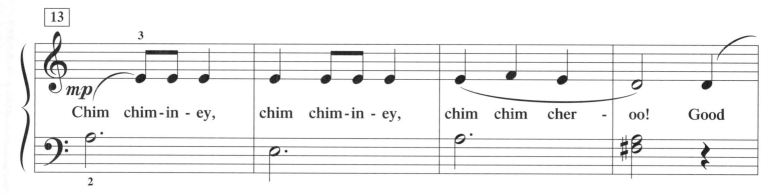

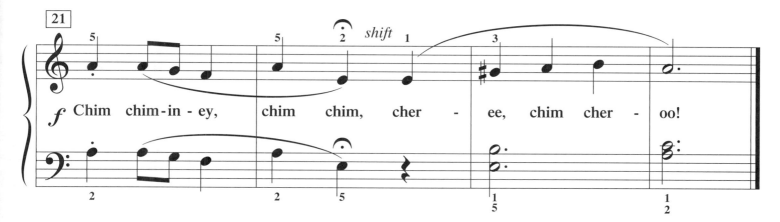

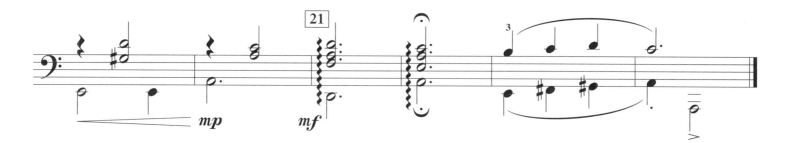

FF3041

WHO SAID THIS?
On a scale from one to ten,
YOU are an ELEVEN!

A Whole New World

from *ALADDIN*

Music by ALAN MENKEN
Lyrics by TIM RICE

Moderately fast

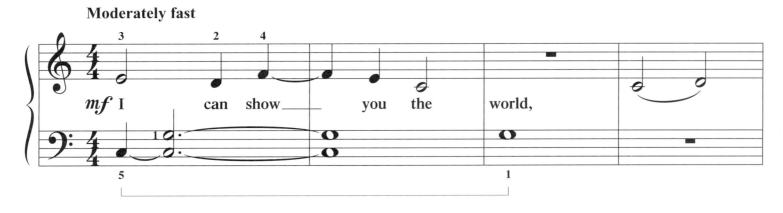

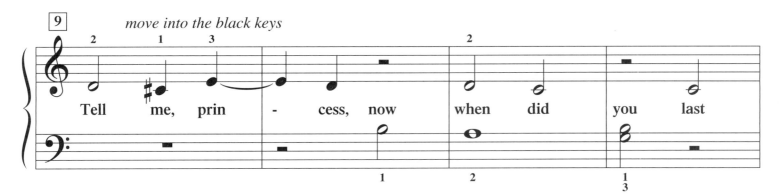

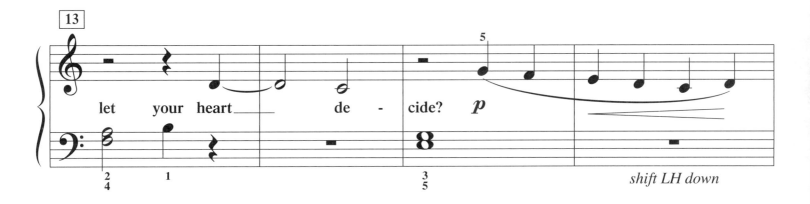

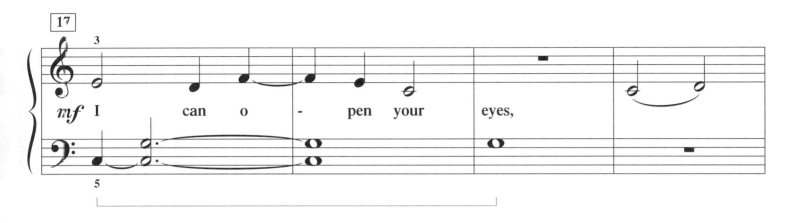

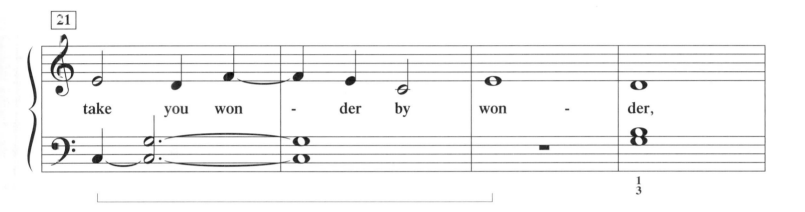

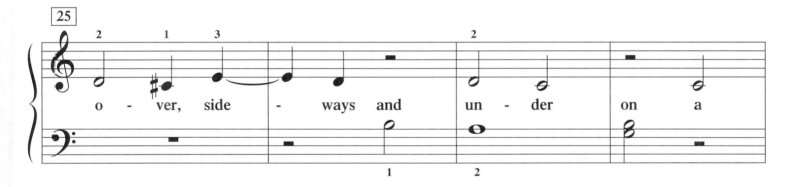

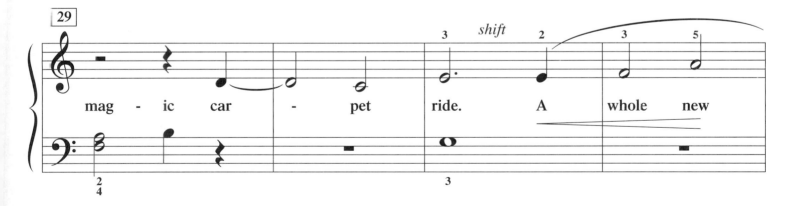

9

FF3041

10

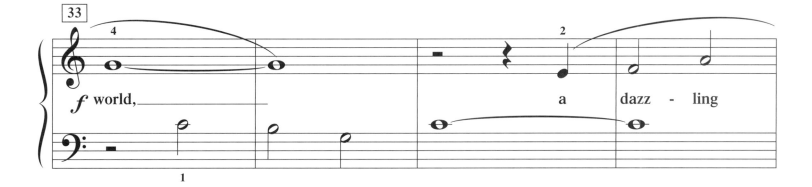

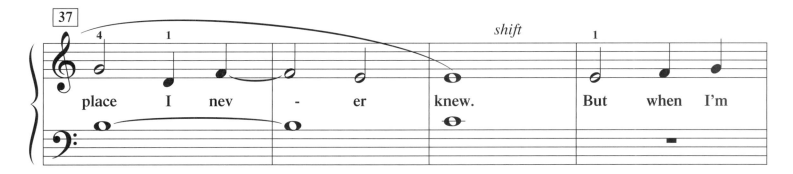

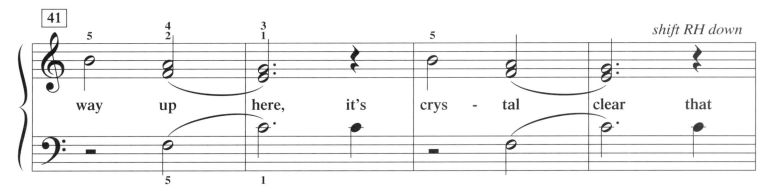

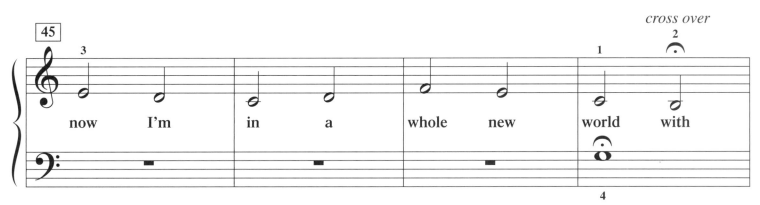

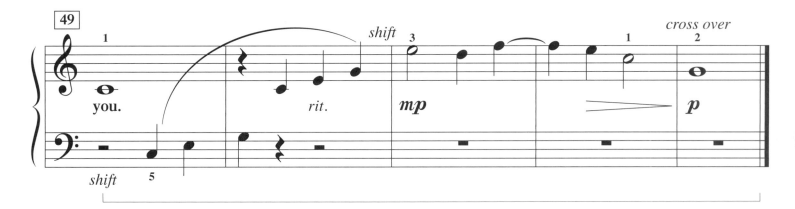

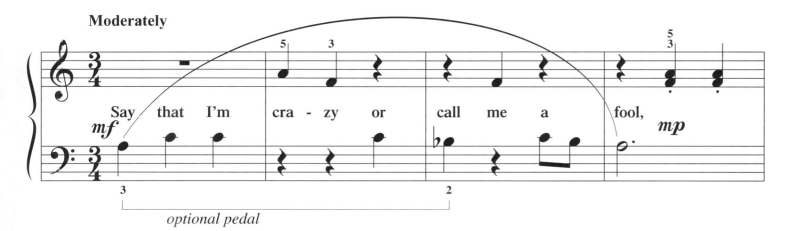

Proud Corazón

from *Coco*

Music by GERMAINE FRANCO
Lyrics by ADRIAN MOLINA

WHO SAID THIS?
Never underestimate
the power of music.

Moderately

Say that I'm cra-zy or call me a fool, *mp*

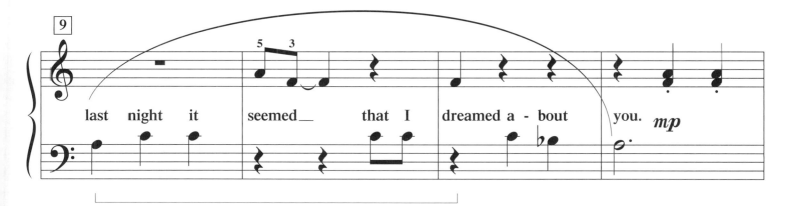

but last night it seemed_ that I dreamed a-bout you. *mp*

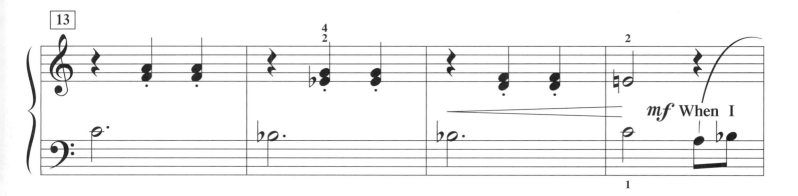

When I

ANSWER: Ernesto de la Cruz

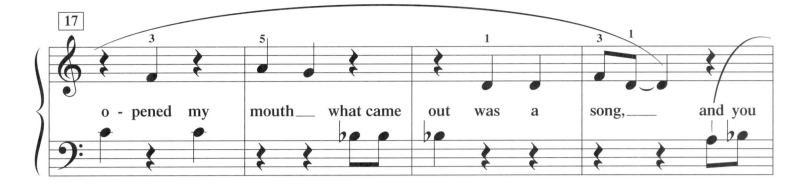

o - pened my mouth___ what came out was a song,___ and you

knew ev - 'ry word___ and we all sang a - long to a

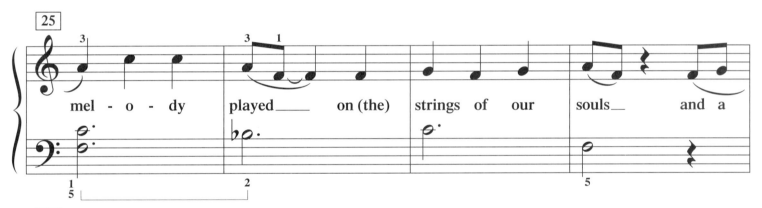

mel - o - dy played___ on (the) strings of our souls___ and a

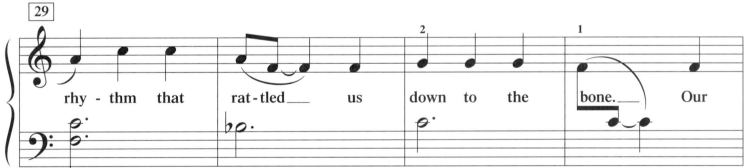

rhy - thm that rat - tled___ us down to the bone.___ Our

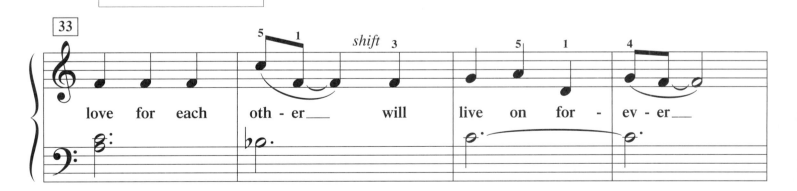

love for each oth - er___ will live on for - ev - er___

FF3041

WHO SAID THIS?
Stop blowing
holes in my ship!

He's a Pirate

from *PIRATES OF THE CARIBBEAN:*
THE CURSE OF THE BLACK PEARL

Music by KLAUS BADELT,
GEOFFREY ZANELLI and HANS ZIMMER

With energy

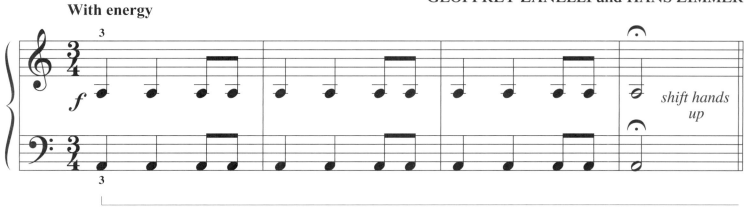

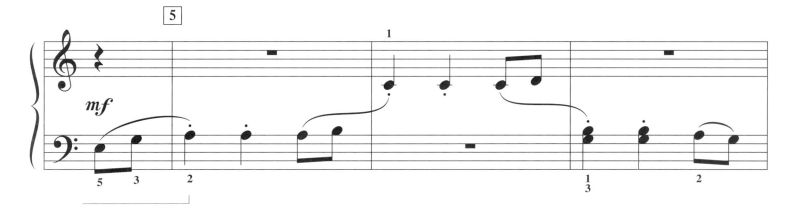

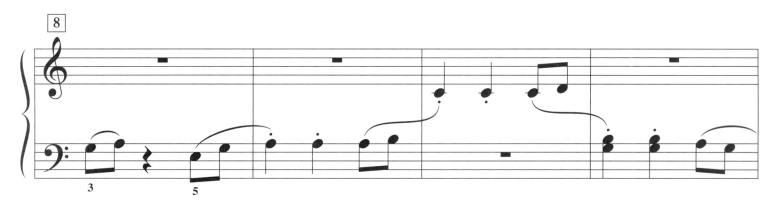

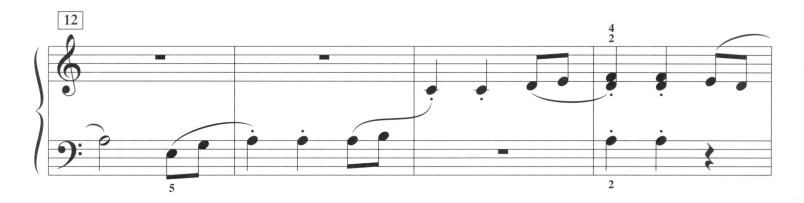

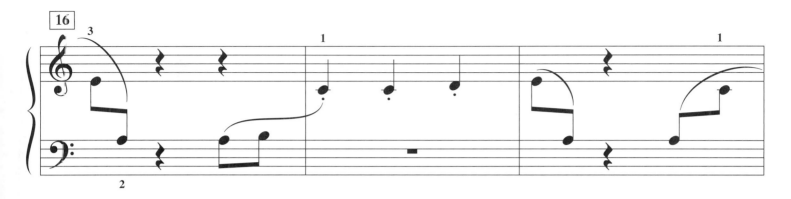

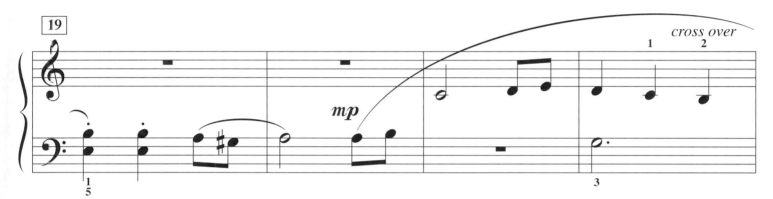

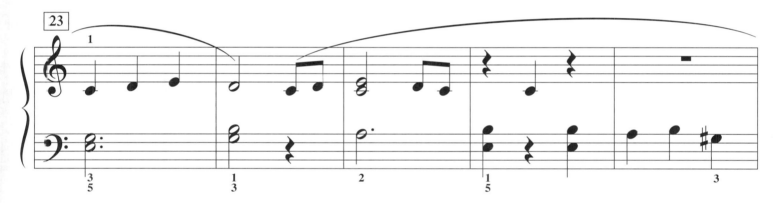

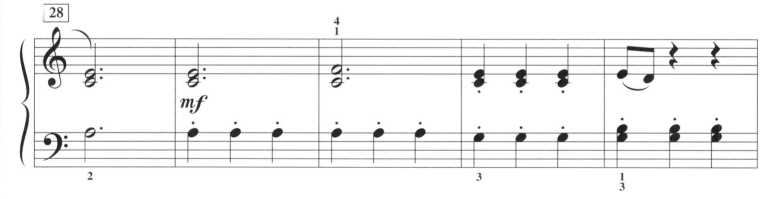

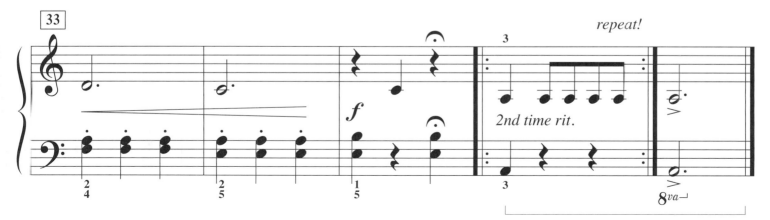

Colors of the Wind

from *POCAHONTAS*

WHO SAID THIS?
Pocahontas, that tree
is talking to me.

Music by ALAN MENKEN
Lyrics by STEPHEN SCHWARTZ

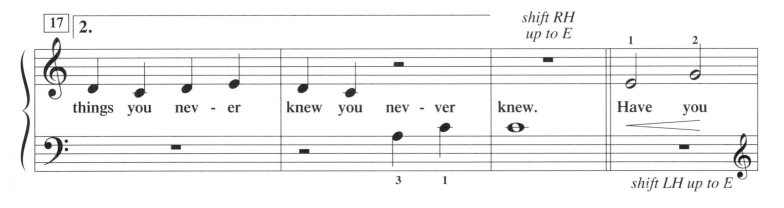

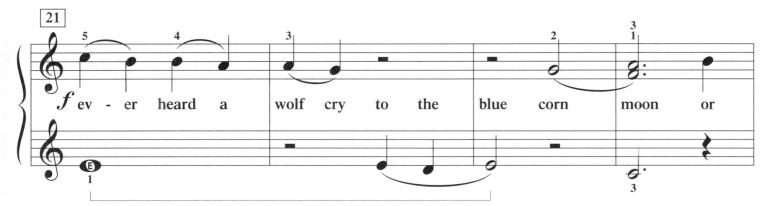

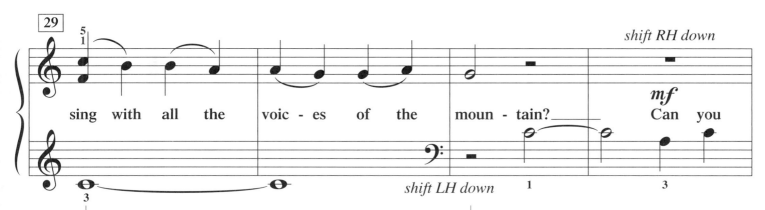

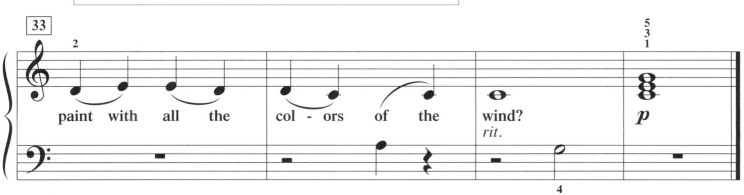

FF3041

Baroque Hoedown

from "*Main Street Electrical Parade*" at
Disneyland® Resort and Magic Kingdom® Park

By JEAN-JACQUES PERREY
and GERSHON KINGSLEY

GET READY!

Ladies and gentlemen, boys and girls. Disneyland proudly presents our spectacular festival pageant of nighttime magic and imagination in thousands of sparkling lights and electro–synthe-magnetic musical sounds. The Main Street Electrical Parade!

Happily

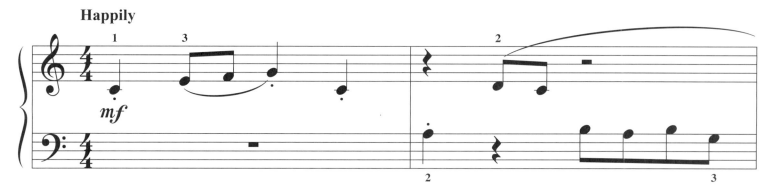

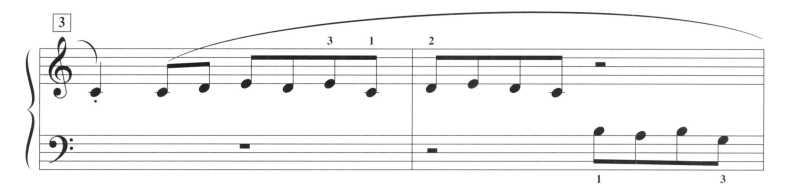

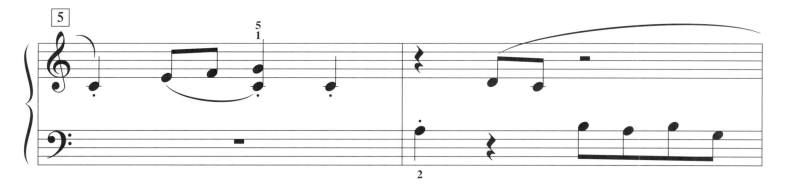

Teacher Duet: (Student plays 1 octave higher)

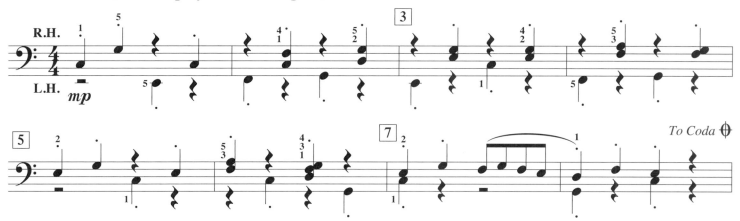

To Coda ⊕

FF3041

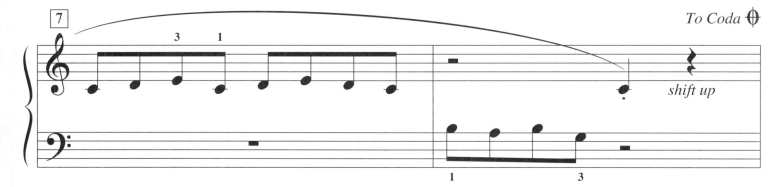

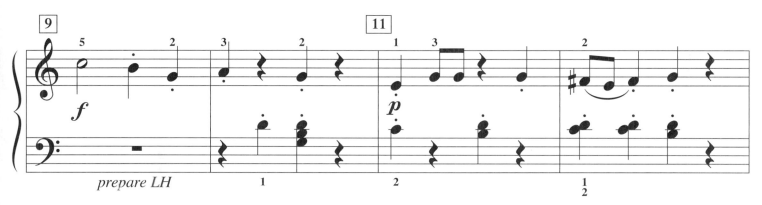

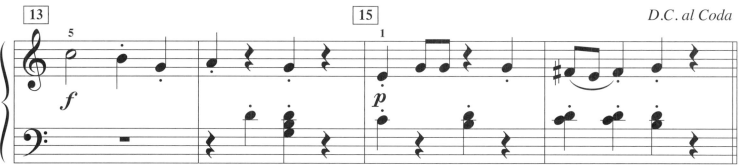

Reflection
from *Mulan*

Music by MATTHEW WILDER
Words by DAVID ZIPPEL

WHO SAID THIS?
You are one lucky bug.
Here, you can sit next to me.

Look at me, I will nev - er pass for a per - fect bride or a per - fect daugh - ter. Can it be I'm not meant to play this part? Now I see That if I were tru - ly to be my - self, I would break my fam - 'ly's heart.

Who is that girl I____ see

WHO SAID THIS?
There's no way I'm kissin' a frog
and eatin' a bug on the same day.

Almost There
from *THE PRINCESS AND THE FROG*

Music and Lyrics by
RANDY NEWMAN

Cheerfully, in swing (8th notes in long-short pattern)

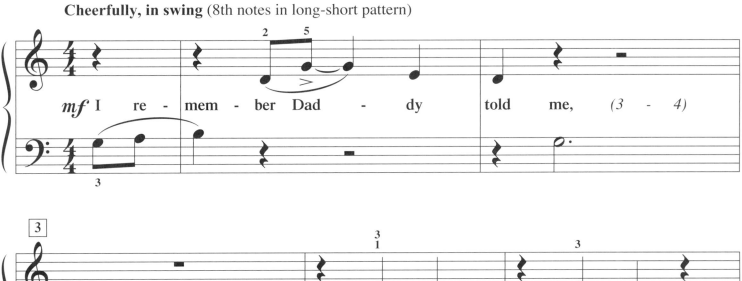

I re - mem - ber Dad - dy told me, *(3 - 4)*

"Fair - y - tales can come true. But you got - ta

Teacher Duet: (Student plays 1 octave higher)

make them hap-pen. It all de-pends__ on you." So I

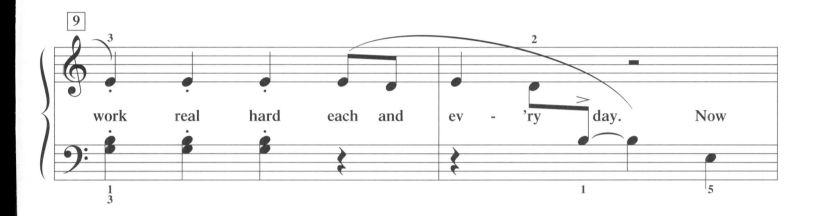

work real hard each and ev - 'ry day. Now

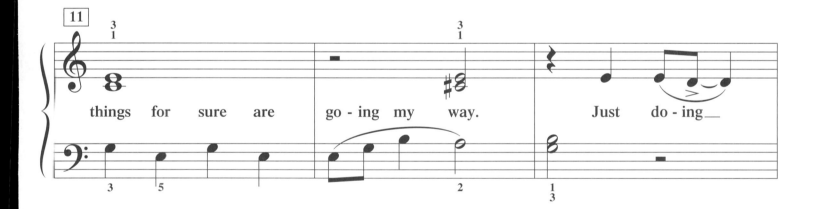

things for sure are go - ing my way. Just do - ing__

what I do.__ Look out__ boys, I'm com - ing through. (And I'm)

cresc.

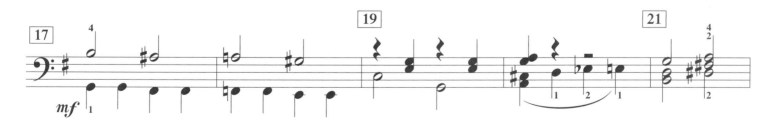